UNCRACKED CODES AND CIPHERS

```
<script type="text/javascript">
<!--
var currentImage = "bigImage1";
var pages = Math.ceil(photos.length / 9);
updatePages();
updateAllImages();
// document.getElementById('bigImage0').src =
// document.getElementById('bigImage0').style.display =
changePhotoDescription( '1' );

function updatePages() {
    var j = 0;

    var html = ' <table style="width: 330px;" cellspacing
```

UNCRACKED CODES AND CIPHERS

ANN BYERS

ROSEN
PUBLISHING®

New York

Published in 2017 by The Rosen Publishing Group, Inc.
29 East 21st Street, New York, NY 10010

First Edition

Library of Congress Cataloging-in-Publication Data

Names: Byers, Ann, author.
Title: Uncracked codes and ciphers / Ann Byers.
Description: First edition. | New York : Rosen Publishing, 2017. | Series: Cryptography : code making and code breaking | Includes bibliographical references and index.
Identifiers: LCCN 2016017678 | ISBN 9781508173106 (library bound)
Subjects: LCSH: Cryptography—History—Juvenile literature. | Ciphers—History—Juvenile literature.
Classification: LCC Z103.3 .B94 2017 | DDC 005.8/2—dc23
LC record available at https://lccn.loc.gov/2016017678

Manufactured in China

CONTENTS

INTRODUCTION

For centuries the pictures carved into stone monuments in Egypt defied analysis. The images of birds, snakes, plants, and other forms had to mean something, but what? The markings, collectively called hieroglyphics, were much like a code. From perhaps the sixth century CE, many people attempted to crack the code. In the 1500s, scholars in Italy, Germany, France, and England pored over reproductions of the inscriptions. But they could not decipher the unusual writing.

When the Rosetta Stone was discovered in 1799, cryptographers—people who unlock hidden messages—thought they had found the key. The broken slab contained three sections of text. One was in hieroglyphics and one in Demotic, a simpler, everyday script that had evolved from the picture writing. The third text was in Greek, a language the cryptographers could read. Guessing correctly that the three sections said the same thing, the cryptographers believed they could match the Greek words with the Egyptian symbols. But twenty-three years after the stone's discovery, the best language experts had figured out only a few of the symbols, mostly proper names. The code seemed impossible. Eventually, however, it was cracked.

A written language such as hieroglyphics is basically a code in which the letters or characters represent sounds or ideas. The scholars solved the puzzle the same way cryptographers today decipher codes. First, they determined the code's language. That language had disappeared hundreds of years earlier. One of the code breakers realized that the Coptic language still

The Rosetta Stone is a slab of black basalt about 3.75 feet (114.5 centimeters) tall. It was inscribed in 196 BCE and probably placed in a temple. It praises the deeds of Ptolemy V of Egypt.

used in some churches was a remnant of ancient Egyptian. That was the first breakthrough. Second, they identified what type of code it was. For well over a thousand years, all the decoders had incorrectly assumed the writing was symbolic; that is, the glyphs (the written characters) communicated ideas. Actually, the glyphs were primarily phonetic, representing sounds. Third, they had the key, the Greek inscription. They were able to crack the seemingly unbreakable code.

A code changes a message by replacing its words with other words, numbers, or signals. The Morse system of dots and dashes is a code. So is sign language. The key to unlocking a code is a codebook that shows the replacements. A cipher hides a message by changing or scrambling the letters in the words. The key to a cipher is a process; that is, the steps used to alter the letters. Different kinds of ciphers have different keys. People often use the words "code" and "cipher" to mean the same thing.

Codes and ciphers can be simple or quite complex. Some messages have baffled the cleverest minds for centuries. Try your hand at some of the most famous codes and ciphers yet to be explained. Who knows? You could be the one to uncover secrets hidden for decades and longer. You might identify a killer or find buried gold!

CHAPTER 1

ANCIENT CODES: THE PHAISTOS DISC AND THE VOYNICH MANUSCRIPT

About 400 miles (650 kilometers) across the Mediterranean from Egypt is the island of Crete. During ancient Egypt's Middle Kingdom, the Minoan culture flourished on the island. Like the Egyptians, the Minoans built large cities with massive palace complexes. Also like the Egyptians, the Minoans developed a system of picture writing. In the early 1900s, when archaeologists discovered the Minoan civilization, they uncovered some of the Minoan writing.

A CURIOUS DISC

High on a hill near the southern coast of Crete, archaeologists found the remains of the large city of Phaistos. In the ruins of what has been called the Phaistos Palace, they recovered two relics with writing in 1908. They are thought to date from about 1700 BCE. One was a stone tablet, similar to some found on other parts of the island. The other, however, was unique.

It was not a stone tablet, but a thin clay disc. It was fairly small, only 6 inches (15 centimeters) in diameter. The writing was on both sides of the disc. The pictures were not carved on the disc as they were on tablets. Someone had pressed seals into the disc when the clay was soft and then fired the disc to harden it.

Forty-five different symbols appear on the Phaistos Disc, many repeated, for a total of about 240 glyphs on the two sides. Some are easily recognized—human figures, birds, animals, plants, tools, and weapons. They were probably read in a clockwise spiral from the outside edge to the center. The glyphs were stamped on the disc, but lines

The most common glyph on the Phaistos Disc is the plumed head, a head with a helmet or crest of straight lines. It appears only next to a vertical line.

were hand carved every so often between symbols. Linguists who have tried to decipher the disc think the lines may group the symbols into words, paragraphs, or some other unit of meaning. The words, if that is what they are, are two to seven glyphs long. One side of the disc has thirty groupings; the other has thirty-one.

But what do they mean? To figure that out, cryptographers need more examples of the writing. Archaeologists know of only one other item with the same symbols. The Arkalokhori axe, found in a cave on Crete, has fifteen glyphs carved into it. Five of the glyphs appear to match five on the Phaistos Disc. Four of those five are also somewhat similar to glyphs of an ancient script called Linear A. A few tablets inscribed with that script have been found throughout Crete, one just inches from the Phaistos disc. Could Linear A tablets be the key to unlocking the disc's code?

Not so far; no one has yet deciphered Linear A. Another Minoan script, called Linear B because it appears to be a later form of Linear A, has not been helpful either. It was decoded in 1952, but no one has been able to link its ninety symbols with the glyphs on the Phaistos Disc.

The disc itself has some clues. The repetition of glyphs and groups of glyphs led some to think the writing might be a prayer, a hymn, or a story. Some think it could be a list of some kind, maybe trade items. The thirty groupings on one side and thirty-one on the other suggest something related to a calendar. Another idea is that the disc is a game board similar to rectangular boards found among other ancient cultures. The truth is waiting to be discovered.

More than one thousand tablets like this one with Linear A writing have been found in Crete and in other parts of Greece as well as in Turkey and Israel.

THE VOYNICH MANUSCRIPT

The Phaistos Disc is hard to decipher because it has little information, only forty-five symbols. Another very old relic has not been deciphered is the Voynich Manuscript, even though it has only about 240 pages! The unusual book had gathered dust in a European library for three hundred years. IThe book is called the Voynich Manuscript after a London book dealer who purchased it in 1921.

Wilfrid Voynich found a letter inside the book dated 1666. The letter claimed the book once belonged to Holy Roman Emperor Rudolf II (1552–1612), who gave it to the person in charge of his gardens, who

WIG WAG

American Civil War soldiers used a code called Wig Wag. The soldiers stood on high ground or raised platforms and waved huge flags or lanterns in specific ways to signal letters of the alphabet. The flags and lights could be seen for miles, so Wig Wag was a good form of battlefield communication. But the signs could also be seen by the enemy. A Union officer developed the code, and his assistant went to the Confederate side, taking his knowledge of the signals with him. So both armies had to encipher their codes; they had to scramble the letters. They drew two alphabet discs and matched letters on one disc to different letters on the other. By rotating one disc, they could change the cipher. Civil War code breakers were good, so the ciphers had to be changed often!

Union soldiers of the Signal Corps sent Wig Wag messages from atop the tower at this station in Virginia in 1864.

was also a pharmacist and chemist. But the manuscript was nearly two hundred years old when the emperor bought it; scientists who tested the paper and the ink have said the book was made between 1404 and 1438. The man who wrote the letter couldn't read the book, so he sent it to a German professor, hoping he could decipher it. The book made its way over the centuries to many scholars in several countries, but none have made sense of the very strange markings.

The Voynich Manuscript is full of illustrations. The different pictures appear to divide the book into six sections. The first part, about half the book, seems to be about herbs. There are large drawings of plants and plant parts. Some look realistic and some seem quite imaginary. None look like any known plant. An astronomy section has images of the sun, moon, stars, and signs of the zodiac. Another section has a variety of circular designs. The strangest drawings are in the biological section: naked people in various poses and groups amid tubes and clouds. The fifth section, with drawings of jars and plant leaves and roots, looks like a pharmaceutical, or drug, manual.

The last section is almost entirely text. Other sections also have what appear to be paragraphs of text. Text appears with some of the illustrations, probably labeling the pictures. But the script does not look like any known form of writing. It looks like an alphabet with twenty to twenty-five letters. Five places have Latin text in the margins, but they have not helped cryptographers decipher the unusual characters.

In almost four hundred years, the manuscript has been examined by many experts in science, art, languages, mathematics, and cryptography. William Friedman, an acclaimed American cryptographer, put

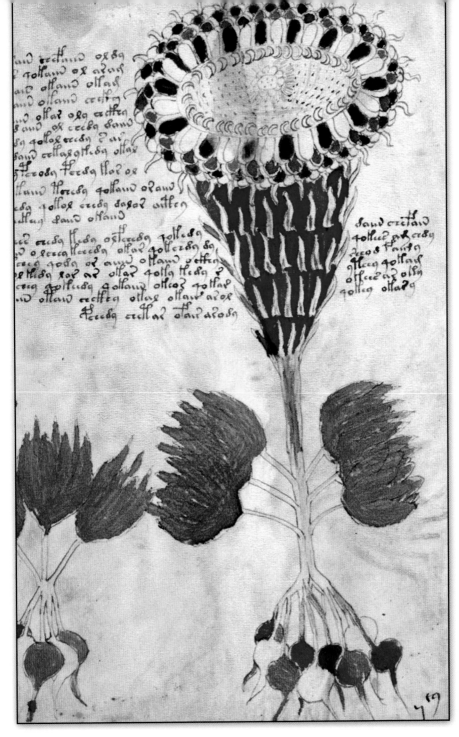

This page from the Herb section of the Voynich Manuscript shows the script that appears throughout the book and the unusual nature of the images.

together a study group of some of the best code breakers of the twenti-eth century. Today, code breakers use computers to analyze patterns in the writing.

Some analysts think the script is an unusual alphabet, perhaps some kind of Greek or Latin shorthand. Others note that ciphers were popular in the fifteenth century and suggest that the script and the pictures may be someone's creative puzzle. Some believe the manu-script was written in a natural language, possibly a language of Asia or of Mesoamerica. They point to the many one-syllable words and a pattern of once- and twice-repeated words.

But all the proposed solutions are only guesses. Perhaps one of the many study groups, websites, and blogs devoted to discussions of possible meanings will eventually solve the four-hundred-year-old mystery.

CHAPTER 2

BURIED TREASURE: THE BEALE PAPERS

Anewer mystery began to unfold in 1885. In that year, a man named James B. Ward published a pamphlet with an intriguing story. He wrote about an adventurer named Thomas Jefferson Beale who traveled with a few friends to "the great Western plain," where they found $40 million in gold and silver. Thinking their treasure was not safe in the Wild West, they buried it somewhere near the town of Bufords in Bedford County, Virginia, in 1819. Then they returned to dig for more gold.

The men worried that if something happened to them out West their families

A man stands on Sharptop Peak in Bedford County, Virginia, an area of mountains and caves that might, or might not, conceal buried treasure.

would not be able to find the secret stash. How could they hide the fortune from the world but allow their relatives to find it? Beale devised an elaborate solution. He enciphered three documents describing the treasure, telling where it was hidden, and listing the names of the men to whom it belonged. He entrusted the documents to a hotelkeeper with instructions to look at them only if no one returned to reclaim them in ten years. He put the key to the ciphers in an envelope addressed to the hotelkeeper. He left that envelope with someone in St. Louis, to be mailed in ten years.

Ten years passed. No one came for the papers and no key arrived at the hotel. The hotelkeeper could not decipher the documents and they wound up with Ward. At least that is the story he told more than sixty years after the treasure was buried. When Ward could decipher only one of the three papers, he published all three and invited anyone who wished to look for the gold to have a go at it.

THE CIPHER

Each of the three documents contained a series of numbers, from one to three digits in length. The first part of Paper #2 begins this way:

115, 73, 24, 807, 37, 52, 49, 17, 31, 62, 647, 22, 7, 15

Ward reasoned that the numbers constituted a multiple substitution code—each number was a substitute for a letter. In this type of code, the key is a codebook. Every word in the codebook is numbered, and the message is encoded by deciding which letter of the word in the codebook is to be substituted for the letter in the plaintext—the real message.

GEORGE WASHINGTON'S CODEBOOK

One of the reasons George Washington was able to defeat the vastly superior British army was the Culper Spy Ring. His spies kept him informed about the numbers and movements of enemy soldiers. After the British intercepted some of Major Benjamin Tallmadge's letters, the major realized the spies needed to encrypt their communications. Tallmadge came up with a code using the 1777 edition of *Entick's Spelling Dictionary*.

In a typical dictionary code, the plaintext word is located in the dictionary and the word is converted into a number corresponding to its page in the dictionary and location on the page. Tallmadge added some elements, but Washington's codebook was basically a dictionary. The spies also used invisible ink, sometimes writing between the lines of ordinary letters and shopping lists. Historians believe none of the Culper Ring's messages were ever decrypted.

Benjamin Tallmadge is deemed the first director of American intelligence. He led the Culper Spy Ring that had a role in capturing Benedict Arnold.

Ward said he tried using many different books, poems, and texts as the codebook and eventually discovered the key: the Declaration of Independence. The first letter of the key word was substituted for the letter of the plaintext. For the coded line above: The 115th word of the Declaration is "instituted," so the first letter is "i." the 73rd word is "hold," so the second letter is "h." Following the key, the line reads, "I have deposited . . ."

CRACKING THE CODE

Ward had decoded Paper #2. In it Beale said he had buried eight thousand pounds of gold and silver and $13,000 in jewels in iron pots

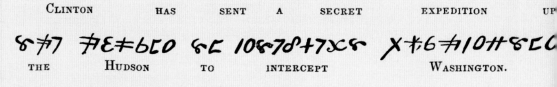

CLINTON	HAS	SENT	A	SECRET	EXPEDITION	UP
THE	HUDSON	TO	INTERCEPT	WASHINGTON.		

Washington's code book used alphabet substitution. Note, for example, the same endings for "Clinton," "Hudson," and "Washington" and the same symbol replacing H in several words.

about 4 miles (6.4 km) from the town of Bufords. Paper #1 gave the exact location and Paper #3 listed the names of the people in Beale's party. But the Declaration of Independence was not the codebook for the other two papers. Ward tried other historical documents, passages from the Bible, lines from Shakespeare's plays, but he could not find the key. After years without success, he published his pamphlet with the story, letters from Beale, Paper #2 and his solution, and the unsolved papers.

Over the course of the next 130 years, hundreds of people have tried to break the code. Many have claimed to know where the treasure is buried. People have traipsed all over the area with Geiger counters, magnetometers, and metal detectors. Some have dynamited or bull-dozed gaping holes in the ground around Bufords. For almost thirty years (1968–1996) the Beale Cipher Association conducted semi-nars and exchanged ideas about the coded messages. So far, no one has found iron pots of gold.

TRUE OR FALSE?

Is there buried treasure or are the Beale Papers an elaborate hoax? Are Papers #1 and 3 real messages or gibberish? A computer analysis of the documents shows patterns that look like real messages in the same type of code as Paper #2 but with a different key. But there is plenty of evidence to suggest that Ward might have made up the whole story.

Careful analysis of word and punctuation patterns shows that the story in the pamphlet, written by Ward, and the letters, supposedly written by Beale, could very well have been the work of the same person.

Also, certain words in the letters, dated in the 1820s, were not used in other writing until the 1840s.

Then there is the name Thomas Jefferson Beale. The census records have no listing of a Thomas Beale living anywhere near Bedford County in the 1700s or 1800s. If the papers are a hoax, Ward may have chosen the name Thomas Jefferson after the president who invented a cipher wheel, encoded many of his official messages, and penned the Declaration used as the key to Paper #2. "Beale" could have been a reference to Ned Beale, the man who announced the California gold rush when he brought the first samples of the gold to the East in 1848.

Whether the story is true or false, people continue to try to decode the documents. One man insisted the papers say that Beale's friends were murdered and the treasure was dug up. Some believe the US National Security Agency solved the code and took the gold. Even if the story turns out to be a hoax and there is no treasure, many professional and amateur cryptologists are curious as to what the uncracked messages say.

A PLAYFUL COMPOSITION: THE DORABELLA CIPHER

S ometimes ciphers are used to conceal information, as with the Beale papers and wartime spies. But sometimes people encrypt messages just for fun—to exercise their creativity or to delight or tease their friends. The communication that has become known as the Dorabella cipher was probably just such a playful message.

THE AUTHOR

The cipher was written by Edward Elgar (1857–1934), a British music composer. Elgar is best known in America for writing the *Pomp and Circumstance* marches, part of which is

Edward Elgar, better known for his musical compositions than his interest in cryptography, wrote his first musical piece for a play he performed around the age of ten.

The score of the first page of Elgar's Enigma Variations *was signed by members of the London Symphony Orchestra, who played the composition in 1901.*

played at many graduation ceremonies. Elgar loved puzzles of all kinds—word plays, word games, and riddles. When a magazine printed a cryptogram its author said was unbreakable, Elgar considered it a challenge. It took Elgar a night without sleep, but he solved the cryptogram.

Elgar incorporated codes into several of his composition. He used note sequences that spelled out names. One of his popular orchestral pieces, *Enigma Variations*, was a musical cipher. He titled it *Variations on a Theme* and said the theme was an enigma—a mystery. Each of the fourteen parts of the music was, he explained, a portrait of one of his friends, and each part was a variation on the mystery theme. Elgar said the theme was something that was well known.

Music lovers are still debating what the enigma might be.

MUSICAL CRYPTOGRAMS

Musical notes, because they have letter names, are easily used in cryptograms. But it takes a very good musician to arrange the notes to produce both clear messages and pleasant sounds at the same time. Some of the most famous composers did just that. They used series of notes or combined the notes into chords. Sometimes the same sequence or chord was used often in a piece, and sometimes the notes were also played in reverse or mixed-up order.

Perhaps the most well-known musical cryptogram was created by Johann Sebastian Bach to spell out his name. In German, the language Bach spoke, the B-flat note is written as B and B-natural is written as H. So Bach "signed" several of his works with the notes B-flat, A, C, B-natural.

The German for E-flat is pronounced "es," so some composers used E-flat for

A 1920 engraving shows the musical notes that correspond to the letters of a poem. The composition is a poem in musical code.

(continued on the next page)

(continued from the previous page)

S. Robert Alexander Schumann, who encrypted his name as E-flat, C, B-natural, A (SCHA, the *A* for Alexander), filled his music with cryptograms. One of his best works, *Carnival*, has the subtitle *Little Scenes on Four Notes*. The composition consists of twenty-one short pieces, and each piece is built on the four notes that make up his name.

One variation was dedicated to Dora Penny. Penny was the daughter of family friends of the Elgars. She was twenty-three in 1897, about seventeen years younger than Elgar. She shared the older man's love of music. Elgar had nicknamed her Dorabella. After visiting with the Pennys for a few days, Elgar wrote a short cipher for Dorabella. He asked his wife to tuck it into the thank-you letter she sent the family.

Penny never figured out the cipher. She kept it in a drawer, forgotten, for forty years. After Elgar died, she published a book about the famous composer. She included the cipher in the appendix. As people read about Elgar and his music, many were intrigued with the unusual message.

THE CIPHER

The cipher was not written in numbers or letters; it was three lines of single, double, and triple semicircles. The glyphs, or symbols, faced eight different directions. The semicircles opened to the top, bottom, left, or right of the page or midway between these points. The cipher looked like a substitution code in which each glyph stood for a letter. Three shapes times eight directions would give twenty-four letters. Code makers often combine *I* with *J* and *U* with *V* so they can write any message with twenty-four letters.

Some cryptographers think Elgar used a pigpen cipher. A pigpen cipher, common in the 1800s, is a code that substitutes symbols for letters. To create a pigpen cipher, the cryptologist draws a grid and inserts letters into the spaces. It is called "pigpen cipher" because the letters are separated like pigs in a pen. The lines of the grid around a letter might be used as the symbol for the letter. A common pigpen cipher is made with a tic-tac-toe grid, an *X*, then another tic-tac-toe grid and another *X*. This configuration has room for twenty-six letters. In the second grid and *X*, some mark such as a dot is added to the letter to distinguish the symbols from those in the first set. The pigpen cipher lends itself to many variations. The different directions of the

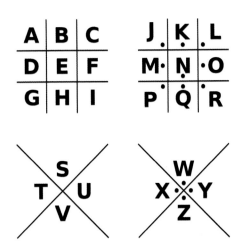

In this example of a pigpen cipher, the letter G would be encoded as a square without the left and bottom lines. P would be the same with a dot in the angle at the upper right.

glyphs in Elgar's variation—if his message is a pigpen cipher—suggest he may have used a circle instead of a grid, maybe a compass.

CLUES

What makes the Dorabella cipher so difficult to solve is its short length. The typical way to decrypt a substitution cipher is frequency analysis. That is, cryptographers figure out which symbols are used most often and match them with the most frequently used letters of the language. The decoders also look for common letter patterns, like *th* or *ing*. But the eighty-seven glyphs of the Dorabella cipher were too few for frequency analysis.

If cryptographers know the relationship between the sender and the receiver of the message, they can search for certain words. For example, a communication from wartime spies might have the word "attack" and drug dealers might use words like "goods," "money," or "shipment." With the Dorabella cipher, however, no one had any idea what Elgar would want to tell his young friend.

Elgar left some clues; he drew the same unusual squiggles in three other places. The semicircles first appeared ten years earlier, on a program for a concert the composer attended. The cipher was just a short line, eighteen glyphs, jotted in the margin of the program; again, too brief for analysis. The second instance came just a year before the note to Dorabella. When Elgar solved the "uncrackable" cipher challenge from the magazine, he described how he arrived at the solution on three cards called "courage cards." One of the cards contained ten of the curious shapes, but no explanation.

The third clue was more promising. A page from Elgar's notebook, written twenty-three years after the Dorabella cipher, actually has a key. It has drawings of a circle with lines inside that show how he probably positioned letters before converting them to semicircles. It also has his letters matched to his symbols. On the page, Elgar used the symbols to spell out three messages:

"Marco Elgar," which was the name of his dog;

"a very old cipher";

and "Do you go to London tomorrow?"

But the key in the notebook did not unlock the Dorabella cipher.

Some amateur cryptologists have claimed to have found the solution, but the twisted messages they suggest make little sense. The Elgar Society, a group of people interested mainly in Elgar's music, issued a challenge in 2007, the 150th anniversary of Elgar's birth: break the code and receive a prize of fifteen hundred British pounds. The judges thought the responses were interesting but "bizarre." The prize was never claimed, and the cipher is still unsolved.

CHAPTER 4
TWO CHALLENGE CIPHERS

Cash prizes motivate some people, but most amateur cryptologists are drawn to codes and ciphers simply because they are challenging. They love working through tough problems, finding clever patterns, and discovering hidden secrets. Many also enjoy creating puzzles and stumping people. Two such challenge ciphers have become among the most famous uncracked codes.

CHAOCIPHER

One of the unsolved challenges was developed in 1918 by John F. Byrne. He called his system the chaocipher because it made chaos of the language, utterly confusing the order of letters in words. He envisioned his system as a universal system, replacing all other forms of encryption.

The chaocipher consisted of a principle and a device. According to Byrne, the principle was ancient. The device was small—he built it in a cigar box—and so simple a ten-year-old could operate it. In his book *Silent Years*, Byrne boasted that "any person, anywhere, writing any language" could use his principle and his device to encrypt a message that "would be absolutely indecipherable by anyone except the persons for whom the message is intended." Furthermore, if two people encrypted the same plaintext, the coded messages would be entirely different.

John F. Byrne and his son, John Byrne Jr., are pictured here. The elder Byrne entrusted the secret of his chaocipher to the younger, and neither revealed it.

The man who made these claims was not a cryptographer; he was a writer. Byrne had come to New York from Ireland, where he had been a close friend of the far more famous writer James Joyce. Unlike his friend, however, Byrne had little success selling his writing. Nor was he able to sell his chaocipher.

No Takers

Before offering his system to the world, Byrne took his homemade device to a patent attorney. The lawyer was impressed with what the device could do, but he said it looked like a toy. He suggested that Byrne have someone make a more professional model. Unfortunately, Byrne could not afford that expense.

A friend thought the US State Department might be interested in Byrne's device. But the secretary of state did not need a new encryption method. Byrne tried to demonstrate his chaocipher to the War Department, but the military officers rejected it. When he heard the navy wanted to develop a cryptography system, Byrne sent a proposal. This too was dismissed. No government agency wanted the device.

Neither did any business. Byrne tried unsuccessfully to convince corporations such as American Telephone and Telegraph Company (ATT) that the chaocipher would enable them to protect company secrets. Frustrated, he turned to the general public.

THE CHALLENGE CIPHER

In 1953, Byrne published *Silent Years: An Autobiography with Memoirs of James Joyce and Our Ireland.* The last chapter was all about the chaocipher. It described the history of his invention and his attempts to offer it to government departments. The chapter included twenty-three pages of plaintext and corresponding ciphertext encrypted with the chaocipher. The book ended with a challenge cipher—the following two lines of text and an offer of five thousand dollars to the first person who could decipher them.

HCYXR XRZWN TXOAI MOWEK PSIXP CPOLZ JJMXS CYLRF UKMYF DPRCOARREU

DGYQH TQCFJ NGNQA DTLBU MYVDM ULXIW XNVHG OIK

Byrne wanted people to try to crack his code so he could prove it was indecipherable. He sent a copy of his book to Albert Einstein and suggested it "might

There is no record of Albert Einstein responding to Byrne's cipher challenge, but he must have read it because he marked paragraphs in his copy of Byrne's book.

be of scientific interest" to the renowned mathematician. For nearly sixty years many cryptologists puzzled over the nineteen blocks of letters, but none solved the challenge.

THE ANSWER

John Byrne died in 1960 with his device lost and his principle still undiscovered. His son knew how his father's system worked, and he constructed a crude model of the original device from cardboard and wooden tiles. But he also died without disclosing the key to the cipher. Fortunately for code analysts, his widow donated the little model as well as all his papers on the cipher to the National Cryptologic Museum in 2012. The challenge cipher was never cracked, but its secret was revealed.

The chaocipher is a complex substitution cipher. Byrne's device consists of two different alphabet wheels, one for the plaintext and one for the ciphertext. The wheels connect so that as one rotates clockwise the other turns counterclockwise. Every time a plaintext letter is matched with a ciphertext letter, the two letters are moved to new slots in the wheels and all the other letters shift one space. This process makes the code unique every time it is used.

Byrne was right when he said a ten-year-old could encrypt with his machine. What about his other claim— that the messages would be "absolutely indecipherable" by anyone except the intended recipients? Cryptographers are still working to see if that is true.

Unseen Heroes Help Crack the Enigma

The Enigma machine was the pride of German intelligence in World War II. It used rotors, switches, plugs, and circuits arranged in a number of different orders to create fifteen million million possible ways to encrypt a message! For extra security, the settings on the machine were changed every day, further multiplying the number of possibilities.

Alan Turing's development of the bombe, an early computer, enabled British cryptanalysts to test intercepted messages against some of those possibilities. Each bombe mirrored the workings of thirty-six Enigma machines. Every day the 108 drums on the front of each bombe were turned to correspond to potential Enigma rotor settings. All the plugs in the back of the machine were rearranged. Two thousand to six thousand messages were fed into the machine, and possibilities were eliminated until the code for that day was broken. Everything had to be exact—numbers accurate, wires brushed, plugs tight and straight.

The mundane work of deciphering Enigma-encrypted messages was performed by an army of Wrens, young women of the Women's Royal Naval Service. They operated the bombes around the clock in eight-hour shifts. Historians estimate that their service shortened the war by two years.

D'AGAPEYEFF CHALLENGE CIPHER

Cryptographers are also still working on another challenge cipher from about the same time. The cipher was crafted by a man well versed in the art of cryptography. Alexander D'Agapeyeff was a Russian-born British citizen who had been an intelligence officer in the Royal Army. He was involved with spy and counterspy activities between Germany and Russia during and after World War I. In the 1930s another war was looming and people were interested in secret messages. Oxford University Press asked D'Agapeyeff to write a book on the subject. He published *Codes and Ciphers* in 1939, a how-to of cryptography. It described the history of the art, gave examples of different types of codes and ciphers, and explained how to solve them. On the last page D'Agapeyeff printed a challenge cipher and invited readers to solve it. The cipher was a set of seventy-nine five-number blocks. The first line looked like this:

75628 28591 62916 48164 91748 58464 74748 28483 81638 18174

In this simple Polybius square, S is encoded as 43. Thus the word "spy" would be 43 35 54.

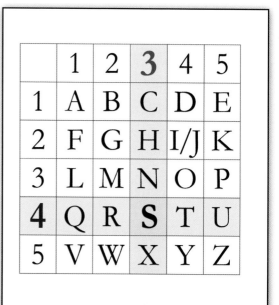

	1	2	3	4	5
1	A	B	C	D	E
2	F	G	H	I/J	K
3	L	M	N	O	P
4	Q	R	S	T	U
5	V	W	X	Y	Z

Professional and amateur code breakers went to work on the challenge. Most assumed the cipher was one of the many D'Agapeyeff explained in the book. One fact about the cipher that was obvious to several who attempted to crack it was that if the numbers were regrouped as pairs a pattern emerged. The first number in each pair was a digit from 6 to 9 and the second number was a digit from 1 to 5. This suggested a grid cipher—more specifically, a Polybius square.

Named for an ancient Greek historian, a Polybius square is constructed by writing the letters of the alphabet in a five-by-five grid, usually combining *I* and *J*. The grid looks a little like a game board, so the encryption method is sometimes called a checkerboard cipher. Each letter is given a two-digit name according to where it is in the grid; the first digit is the number of the row and the second digit is the number of the column.

D'Agapeyeff was much too sophisticated a cryptographer to use such a primitive type of cipher without adding other layers of encryption. Perhaps he began with a Polybius cipher then inserted extra letters as he described in one section of his book. Maybe he scrambled the coded letters. He might have made mistakes when he performed the coding. Or maybe it wasn't a checkerboard cipher at all.

Ten years after the challenge was given, the cipher was still a mystery. Frustrated code breakers finally gave up and asked D'Agapeyeff for the solution. The author had forgotten how he had created the cipher and what it said! When *Codes and Ciphers* was reprinted in 1952, the challenge cipher was not in it. But old copies were available, and with today's technology anyone can find the D'Agapeyeff cipher on the internet and try to crack the still-unsolved puzzle.

CHAPTER 5

A KILLER'S CIPHERS: THE ZODIAC

C hallenge ciphers are fun and entertaining, but some ciphers are deadly serious. Such was the case with four cryptic notes from a man calling himself Zodiac. The ciphers were part of a total of twenty letters Zodiac mailed to police agencies and newspapers in the San Francisco Bay Area from 1968 to 1974. In them he claimed responsibility for thirty-seven murders and dared the authorities to find him.

THE FIRST LETTERS

The first communication arrived in the mail on August 1, 1969. The writer identified himself as the murderer of three people: two teenagers who had been killed seven months earlier and a girl slain four weeks prior to the letter. He included facts about both incidents that had not been made public. The same letter was sent to three Bay Area newspapers. In each letter was one part of a three-part cipher and the following demand, complete with misspellings:

I want you to print this cipher on the front page of your paper. In this cipher is my idenity. If you do not print this cipher by the afternoon of Fry. 1st of Aug 69, I will go on a kill ram-Page Fry. night. I will cruse around all weekend killing lone people in the night then move on to kill again, until I end up with a dozen people over the weekend.

All three letters were signed the same way: with a cross drawn through a circle.

When the *San Francisco Chronicle* printed its third of the cipher, it also printed an article saying the police were not sure the letter was really from

Inside this card, sent by Zodiac to the San Francisco Chronicle *on November 8, 1969, was the 340 cipher, which is still unsolved.*

the murderer. The police would need another letter with more facts to be convinced.

The killer obliged. On August 4 the *San Francisco Examiner* received a letter that began "This is the Zodiac speaking." It was definitely from the murderer; it described the crimes in chilling detail and was signed with the same crossed circle. With the killer's name revealed, the symbol made some sense; it was the logo of the Zodiac Watch Company.

The writer suggested that solving the cipher from the previous letter would enable the authorities to catch him. He wrote, "Are the police having a good time with the code? . . . When they do crack it they will have me."

THE 408 CIPHER

The code consisted of 408 handwritten characters—letters, backward letters, shapes, and symbols. Each of the three parts had eight lines with seventeen glyphs on each line. The complete cipher was printed in the newspapers, and it was solved within a week. The police had sent the cipher to professional cryptographers at a Bay Area navy base, but they were not the ones to figure it out. The code was cracked by a high school history teacher and his wife, Donald and Bettye Harden.

The message was a homophonic substitution cipher. In a simple substitution cipher the same symbol is substituted for a letter every time that letter appears in the plaintext. In a homophonic substitution cipher, a few of the letters are represented in the ciphertext by more than one symbol. The letters with the multiple substitutions are usually frequently used letters such as *E* and *T*. Zodiac used twelve different glyphs for the letter *E*.

The Hardens attacked the 408 cipher by assuming it would contain the word "kill." They were correct; the word appeared four times in the message. They looked for repeated pairs of symbols that might be *LL*. In front of some of the repeated pairs was a triangle, which they guessed was a substitution for *I*. The same triangle was the first character in the cipher, and starting a message with *I* made sense. From there, the couple plodded through many possibilities. A number of misspellings, probably intentional, complicated their efforts, but after more than twenty hours they had decrypted all but the last eighteen symbols. The

This cipher key has the first few lines of Zodiac's 408 cipher and the letters the Hardens determined made up the plaintext.

DECRYPTION CONVICTS A TERRORIST

Rajib Karim's coworkers at British Airways were stunned when government agents arrested Karim at his desk. His neighbors did not know why police cars sat outside Karim's home for three days. A year later they all learned that the man they had known for three years was actively plotting to plant a bomb aboard a British plane.

Even the British counterterrorism officers had not known exactly what he was up to until they got hold of his computer. There they found three hundred messages to the radical Anwar al-Alwaki and other terrorists. But the messages were encrypted. Detectives struggled for nine months before they finally broke the codes. They told the *Telegraph* it was "the most sophisticated encryption ever seen in international terrorism." Karim had hidden his messages inside eight layers of encryption; the cryptographers likened it to a set of Russian nesting dolls.

But beneath all those layers his system was the oldest and simplest of all codes: a Caesar cipher. A Caesar cipher is a substitution cipher that keeps the alphabet in order, merely shifting all the letters one or more positions. When the detectives got to the actual ciphertexts, they finally had the evidence that convicted Karim of four terrorism charges. In March 2011 he was sentenced to thirty years in prison.

cipher was simply a rambling message telling how much the Zodiac liked killing people. It did not reveal his identity.

The code for the final 18 glyphs of the 408 cipher has never been solved. Some people think it is homophonic substitution like the rest of the cipher but with the symbols representing different letters. Many think, or at least hope, the characters contain the Zodiac's name. Solutions have been proposed, but none have been accepted as accurate by experts. A number of cryptographers believe the figures are meaningless fillers, inserted to even out the message so all three parts of the cipher have the same number and arrangement of symbols.

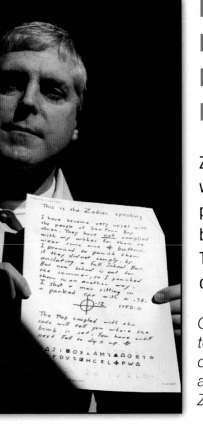

MORE MURDERS, MORE MESSAGES

Zodiac did not go on the weekend killing rampage he had promised, but he did strike again. The authorities are certain he committed

Chicago Police lieutenant John Lewison claims to have solved a cipher telling where Zodiac hid a bomb.

or attempted seven murders, and they suspect him of several other unsolved killings. He continued to write, touting his cleverness and making fun of the police who could not catch him. A June 1970 letter ended with "Zodiac = 12; SFPD [San Francisco Police Department] = 0." Subsequent letters upped the score: Zodiac = 13, then 17+, and in January 1974 he claimed 37 murders.

After the three-part cipher, three more letters contained ciphers using the same symbols as the 408. Two were very brief; one with only thirty-two characters professed to conceal the location of a bomb. Another said, "My name is" followed by thirteen glyphs. These were too short for code breakers to figure out. But one, sent November 8, 1969, shortly after the last of the confirmed murders, filled an entire page with 340 symbols.

The Zodiac 340 cipher is one of the most puzzling unsolved codes. It looks much like the 408 cipher, with neat rows of seventeen glyphs each. But the substitution—if it is also a substitution cipher—is not the same. The 408 has fifty-four unique symbols and the 340 has sixty-two. Despite years of work by some of the best cryptologists in the nation, including in the Federal Bureau of Investigation (FBI), the cipher remains a mystery.

The murders also are still unsolved. Police officers questioned several suspects, but they could not prove any of them was the killer. Different amateur sleuths claim to have found different names in the Zodiac's symbols, but none of their solutions appear convincing to law enforcement. The investigation is no longer active, but the case remains open. Solving the 340 cipher could close the case.

CHALLENGING THE EXPERTS: THE KRYPTOS MONUMENT

S ome of the best code breakers in the world work in the Central Intelligence Agency (CIA). When the agency began planning for a new headquarters building for its campus in Langley, Virginia, the designers decided to include some artwork on the grounds. They wanted a large sculpture that was attractive and also reflected the challenging work of gathering and analyzing critical pieces of intelligence. From all the artists who submitted designs, they selected Jim Sanborn.

Sanborn is a professional artist who has received numerous awards and commissions for his work. He has exhibited in major museums in the United States, Asia, and Europe. He is a man of many

Sculptor Jim Sanborn poses in 2003, thirteen years after the Kryptos Monument was erected.

interests. In addition to earning bachelor's and master's degrees in art, Sanborn studied archaeology, paleontology, and social anthropology. Many of his sculptures deal with hidden things—unseen forces of nature such as magnetism and atomic energy, ancient and foreign writing, and encoded texts. The piece he proposed for the CIA was called *Kryptos*, the Greek word for "hidden" or "secret."

THE MONUMENT

Sanborn does not simply sculpt imaginative forms. He researches his subjects thoroughly so the finished artwork is full of meaning. In designing *Kryptos*, Sanborn spent countless hours studying the history of communication, intelligence gathering, and cryptography. The finished product, erected in 1990, shows the fruit of that study. The artwork consists of several parts. One part is a set of granite slabs and copper plates inscribed with ancient ciphers and Morse code. One piece of granite has a compass etched into it, and nearby is a lodestone, a

The Vigènere tableau on the Kryptos *sculpture has 867 letters. Most lines consist of the alphabet minus the letters in "Kryptos" along with the word "Kryptos."*

magnetic rock. The main part is a 12-foot-high (3.6-meter) *S*-shaped scroll of copperplate. The scroll unfurls from a pole of petrified wood and wraps around a pool of bubbling water. The copperplate scroll is completely covered with cutouts of 1,735 letters.

Sanborn explained that the petrified wood represents the trees that were removed to make room for the sculpture. Trees are the sources of bark and paper, and thus they symbolize the beginning of written communication. Sanborn meant for the bubbling pool to remind the viewer that information is continually being produced and given out, and no one can tell exactly where it may go. The cutout letters, the most obvious feature of the monument, point to the heart of the CIA's mission. They form a mystery, written in cipher, a hidden message challenging the experts to uncover its meaning.

THE CIPHERS

Actually, the *Kryptos* scroll contains four ciphers. Cryptographers have labeled them K1, K2, K3, and K4. Sanborn wrote the plaintexts with the help of a writer. To encode the plaintexts, he worked with a retired CIA cryptographer for four months. Each of the four ciphers has its own code. All the codes in the monument, including the Morse code, have been important in the history of cryptography.

The giant copperplate scroll is divided into two parts. One half has the four ciphers on the front; the other half has to be read from the back. It is a Vigenère tableau, a tool for solving one type of cipher. The tableau, based

Code Talking

In wartime, important messages are frequently intercepted and decrypted. To keep communications secret, officials have to continually change their codes. However, in World War II the US Marines had a code they didn't need to change, a code that was never cracked by the enemy. It was based on the Navajo language.

For some communications, Navajo code talkers could simply relay messages in their native tongue. For others, especially those that included words not found in Navajo, they developed an alphabet code. They listed English words beginning with each letter of the alphabet, mostly names of animals: "bear" for *B*, "cat" for *C*, "dog" for *D*. For each letter, they substituted the Navajo name for the animal or object. For extra security, they used more than one substitution for some letters; for example, the code words for *A* were the Navajo terms for "ant," "apple," and "axe." A code talker could hear a message in English and transmit it over a radio without having to write it down or encipher it; the receiver could translate it back into English immediately. It was the easiest, fastest, and most reliable code the military ever had. About four hundred Navajo code talkers served in World War II.

on the one devised by sixteenth-century French cryptographer Blaise de Vigenère, is basically a chart of alphabets. The Vigenère cipher is created from the tableau and a keyword the encoder chooses. The staff of the CIA and others attempting to decipher the messages assumed that Sanborn's texts were Vigenère ciphers.

CRACKING THE CODES

They were partly right. K1, K2, and K3 used the tableau. But they were not simple Vigenère ciphers. The three had different keywords. One used eight of the alphabets and another used ten. Some of the plaintext words were deliberately misspelled. On top of the Vigenère method of encoding, other encryption systems were added, including a very complex matrix code.

Eight years after the sculpture was unveiled, in 1998, CIA analyst David Stein cracked the first three codes. He spent many of his lunch hours—he estimated about four hundred—poring over the letters with nothing but paper and pencil. He explained his methods and wrote the solution in a paper that was seen only by others in the CIA. A year later, a California computer scientist proclaimed that he had broken the encryption. He had used a computer and arrived at the same solution as Stein.

When the announcement was made in 1999, very few people knew that the code had actually been cracked several years earlier. Cryptographers at the National Security Agency (NSA), the Defense Department's spy agency, had also been interested in the monument.

In 1992, an official at the CIA challenged the expert decoders at NSA to decrypt the ciphers. They not only accepted the challenge, they met it fairly easily. In fact, one NSA analyst figured out K3, the most intricate of the first three ciphers, in about six hours. However, like the people at the CIA, the NSA decoders marked the solution "classified" and kept the news to themselves.

THE UNCRACKED CIPHER

Neither the CIA nor the NSA or anyone else has yet unraveled the last of the four *Kryptos* ciphers. Sanborn said the first three ciphers have clues that will help break the fourth. The plaintext of the first message is a bit mysterious: "Between subtle shading and the absence of light lies the nuance of iqlusion" (the last word is a purposeful misspelling of "illusion"). The second message suggests something is buried within 200 feet (61 m) of the monument. The third is a description of an archaeologist exploring King Tutankhamen's tomb in Egypt. These texts are supposed to help unlock the last cipher.

K4 contains ninety-seven letters. No one has figured out what type of code it is. In 2010, Sanborn offered a clue: the ciphertext letters *NYPVTT* decrypt to the plaintext letters *BERLIN*. In November 2014, the artist gave a second clue: the word after *BERLIN* is *CLOCK*.

So far the clues have been of little help. *Kryptos* websites, chat rooms, and blogs with ideas for decrypting K4 abound. Sanborn receives dozens of letters every week from people claiming to have cracked the code, but no one has. Sanborn warned that the secret of the sculpture will not be revealed until all four ciphers are solved. But even when the K4 code is broken, if it ever is, the mystery may not become clear. The artist has said the message on the monument is a riddle within a riddle.

The *Kryptos* riddle is just one of several that have eluded the best cryptographers. However, like Egyptian hieroglyphics, many codes unbreakable for years have eventually been deciphered. Amateurs as well as professionals have discovered keys that unlock some of the deepest mysteries. With time, effort, new tools, and a little luck, the eight codes described here are just as likely to be cracked.

GLOSSARY

Caesar cipher Substitution cipher created by shifting the entire alphabet one or more positions, forming a cipher alphabet that uses different letters but keeps them in the same order as the plaintext alphabet.

chaos Extreme disorder.

cipher To conceal a message by rearranging letters or words; a message encoded by this method.

code Message whose meaning has been concealed by replacing words with letters, numbers, or symbols.

crypt- Prefix meaning "hidden" or "secret."

cryptography Use of codes and ciphers. Cryptographers write and/or read concealed messages.

de- Prefix meaning "from" or "take out." To decode, decipher, or decrypt is to take the plaintext message out of a ciphertext.

en- Prefix meaning "in." To encode, encipher, or encrypt is to put plaintext into code.

enigma Something difficult to understand. Germany called the machines used for encoding messages during World War II "enigma machines."

frequency analysis Method of breaking a cipher by determining how often specific symbols appear and comparing that frequency with how often specific letters appear in a language.

glyph A written symbol.

homophonic cipher Cipher in which some of the letters are represented in the ciphertext by more than one symbol.

intelligence Information that is useful in making military or political decisions.

linguist A person who studies language and languages.

patent Document that shows who invented an item and protects the inventor from people who try to claim some rights to the item.

pigpen cipher Substitution cipher created by arranging letters in some kind of grid and replacing the letters with symbols connected with the grid.

plaintext A message written in ordinary, easy-to-understand form.

Polybius square Type of substitution cipher that uses an alphabet grid.

relic An object that has survived from an earlier time.

substitution code Code or cipher in which a letter, number, or other symbol is used in place of the original letter.

tableau A dramatic scene or image presented through a grouping of objects.

FOR MORE INFORMATION

American Cryptogram Association
56 Sanders Ranch Road
Moraga, CA 94556-2806
Website: http://cryptogram.org
The American Cryptogram Association is a nonprofit organization that
promotes cryptanalysis as a hobby and an art. Its members include
children and adults and many well-known cryptanalysts. It publishes
the *Cryptogram* magazine. The website has articles, links, and educational resources.

Communications Security Establishment
1500 Bronson Avenue
Ottawa, ON K15 3J5
Canada
(613) 991-8600
Website: https://www.cse-cst.gc.ca
The Communications Security Establishment is the intelligence-gathering and
analysis agency of the government of Canada. It protects the country's
computer networks and information important to its national security.

International Association for Cryptologic Research
Santa Rosa Administrative Center
University of California
Santa Barbara, CA 93106-6120

(805) 893-3072

Website: https://www.iacr.org

The International Association for Cryptologic Research is a nonprofit
scientific organization that promotes research in cryptology. It holds
conferences and workshops and publishes the *Journal of Cryptology*.

International Spy Museum

800 F Street NW

Washington, DC

(202) 393-7798

Website: http://www.spymuseum.org

The International Spy Museum displays artifacts from espionage
activity throughout history and around the world. It has exhibits,
activities, programs, and events that describe the history and
practice of espionage, including code making and breaking.

Khan Academy

1937 Landings Drive

Mountain View, CA 94043

Website: https://www.khanacademy.org

Khan Academy is a nonprofit organization that offers free
online educational videos, tools, and exercises in art,
history, finance, and math. It employs experts in the
different fields to produce the educational materials.
The academy has a number of resources on
cryptography, including a website page: https://
www.khanacademy.org/computing
/computer-science/cryptography/crypt/v/
intro-to-cryptography.

National Cryptologic Museum
9900 Colony Seven Road
Fort Meade, MD 20755
(301) 688-5849
Website: https://www.nsa.gov/about/cryptologic_heritage/museum/index
.shtml
A public arm of the National Security Agency, the National Cryptologic
Museum houses artifacts and exhibits that show the role and impact of
cryptology in the United States and in world history.

WEBSITES

Because of the changing nature of internet links, Rosen Publishing
has developed an online list of websites related to the subject of
this book. This site is updated regularly. Please use this link to
access the list:

http://www.rosenlinks.com/CCMCB/uncrack

For Further Reading

Barber, Nicola. *Who Broke the Wartime Codes?* Portsmouth, NH: Heinemann, 2014.

Bauer, Craig P. *Secret History: The Story of Cryptology*. Boca Raton, FL: CRC Press, 2013.

Charles River editors. *World War II Cryptography: The History of the Efforts to Crack the Secret Codes Used by the Axis and Allies*. North Charleston, SC: CreateSpace, 2016.

Clemens, Raymond, ed. *The Voynich Manuscript*. New Haven, CT: Yale University Press, 2016.

D'Agapeyeff, Alexander. *Codes and Ciphers: A History of Cryptography*. N.p.: Hesperides Press, 2008.

Dooley, John F. *Codes, Ciphers, and Spies: Tales of Military Intelligence in World War I*. New York, NY: Springer, 2016.

Durrett, Deanne. *Unsung Heroes of World War II: The Story of the Navajo Code Talkers*. Lincoln, NE: Bison Books, 2009.

Eldridge, Jim. *Alan Turing*. Seattle, WA: Amazon Digital Services, 2013.

Gortman, Vance. *Uncracked Codes and Ciphers*. Raleigh, NC: Lulu, 2016.

Gregory, Jillian. *Breaking Secret Codes*. North Mankato, MN: Capstone Press, 2011.

Gregory, Jillian. *Making Secret Codes*. North Mankato, MN: Capstone Press, 2011.

Hastings, Max. *The Secret War: Spies, Ciphers, and Guerillas, 1939–1945*. New York, NY: HarperCollins, 2016.

Johnson, Bud. *Break the Code: Cryptography for Beginners.* Mineola, NY: Dover Publications, 2013.

McCartney, Sean. *Breaking the Beale Code.* Ogden, UT: Mountainland Publishing, 2011.

Nez, Chester, and Judith Scheiss Avila. *Code Talker: The First and Only Memoir by One of the Original Navajo Code Talkers of World War II.* Audiobook. Old Saybrook, CT: Tantor Media, 2011.

Simpson, Zed. *The Zodiac Killer: The Mystery of America's Most Infamous Serial Killer.* North Charleston, SC: CreateSpace, 2016.

US Central Intelligence Agency. *Intelligence in the Civil War.* Seattle, WA: Amazon Digital Services, 2016.

van der Bijl, Nicholas. *To Complete the Jigsaw: British Military Intelligence in the First World War.* Gloucestershire, England: History Press, 2015.

Yardley, Herbert O. *The American Black Chamber.* Ebook. Annapolis, MD: Naval Institute Press, 2013.

Weber, Ralph E. *Masked Dispatches: Cryptograms and Cryptology in American History, 1775–1900.* Damascus, MD: Pennyhill Press, 2013.

BIBLIOGRAPHY

Byrne, J. F. *Silent Years: An Autobiography with Memoirs of James Joyce and Our Ireland.* 1953. Chapter 21 (pp. 264–307), reprinted 2009. http://www.mountainvistasoft.com/chaocipher/Silent-Years -Chapter-21-Chaocipher.pdf.

Cartwright, Mike. "Phaistos Disc." *Ancient History Encyclopedia*, June 28, 2012. http://www.ancient.eu/Phaistos_Disk/http://www .ancient.eu/Phaistos_Disk.

Central Intelligence Agency. "Kryptos." July 28, 2014. https://www .cia.gov/about-cia/headquarters-tour/kryptos.

Gardham, Duncan. "British Airways Bomber Jailed for 30 Years." *Telegraph,* March 18, 2011. http://www.telegraph.co.uk/news /uknews/terrorism-in-the-uk/8391162/British-Airways-bomber -jailed-for-30-years.html.

Grinell, Richard. *Zodiac Killer.* Retrieved February 18, 2016. http:// www.zodiacciphers.com.

Heath, Nick. "Hacking the Nazis: The Secret Story of the Women Who Broke Hitler's Codes." *TechRepublic.* Retrieved March 2, 2016. http://www.techrepublic.com/article/the-women-who-helped -crack-nazi-codes-at-bletchley-park.

Hutchinson, Lisa. "Focus on Rajib Karim's Plot to Explode Planes. *Chronicle Live*, February 26, 2013. http://www.chroniclelive.co.uk /news/north-east-news/focus-rajib-karims-plot-explode-1395736.

Jevec, Adam, and Lee Ann Potter. "Memorandum Regarding the Enlistment of Navajo Indians." *Social Education,* vol. 65, no. 5

(September 2001): 262–268. https://www.archives.gov/education/lessons/code-talkers.

Kilmeade, Brian, and Don Yaeger. *George Washington's Secret Six: The Spy Ring that Saved the American Revolution.* New York, NY: Sentinel, 2013.

Museum of Unnatural History. "The Beale Papers," 1885, reprint. Retrieved February 15, 2016. http://www.unmuseum.org/bealepap.htm.

Pelling, Nick. "The D'Agapeyeff Cipher." *Cipher Mysteries,* May 11, 2008. http://www.ciphermysteries.com/2008/05/11/the-dagapeyeff-cipher.

Pelling, Nick. "The Dorabella Cipher and Elgar's *Other* Little Ciphertexts." *Cipher Mysteries,* October 9, 2013. http://www.ciphermysteries.com/2013/10/09/elgars-little-cipher.

Wilcox, Jennifer. *Revolutionary Secrets: Cryptography in the American Revolution.* Fort Meade, MD: Center for Cryptologic History, National Security Agency, 2012. https://www.nsa.gov/about/cryptologic-heritage/historical-figures-publications/publications/pre-wwii/assets/files/Revolutionary_Secrets_2012.pdf.

Zandbergen, Réne. "The Voynich Manuscript." 2016. http://www.voynich.nu/index.html.

Zetter, Kim. "Documents Reveal How the NSA Cracked the Kryptos Sculpture Years Before the CIA." *Wired,* July 10, 2013. http://www.wired.com/2013/07/nsa-cracked-kryptos-before-cia.

Zetter, Kim. "Finally, a New Clue to Solve the CIA's Mysterious Kryptos Sculpture." *Wired*, November 20, 2014. http://www.wired.com /2014/11/second-kryptos-clue.

Zodiackiller.com. "Zodiac Letter and Ciphers." Retrieved February 18, 2016. http://www.zodiackiller.com/Letters.html.

INDEX

ABOUT THE AUTHOR

Ann Byers is a teacher, youth worker, writer, and editor. Although not a cryptographer, she is an avid puzzle solver, enjoying crosswords, cryptograms, cryptoquizzes, and word games of all kinds. She creates ciphers and other word challenges to spice up the lessons she teaches both children and adults.

PHOTO CREDITS

Cover, p. 3 (top) scyther5/Shutterstock.com; cover, p. 3 (bottom) agsandrew/Shutterstock.com; p. 7 Print Collector/Hulton Archive/Getty Images; p. 10 Leemage/Universal Images Group/Getty Images; p. 12 DEA/G. Nimatallah/De Agostini/Getty Image; p. 13 Buyenlarge/Archive Photos/Getty Images; p. 15 Universal History Archive/Universal Images Group/Getty Images; pp. 17, 39, 41 Bettmann/Getty Images; p. 19 Hulton Archive/Archive Photos /Getty Images; p. 20 © North Wind Picture Archives; p. 23 Popperfoto /Getty Images; p. 24 Epics/Hulton Archive/Getty Images; p. 25 © Old Paper Studios/Alamy Stock Photo; p. 27 Anomie/Wikimedia Commons /File:Pigpen cipher key.svg/pd; p. 31 National Cryptologic Museum, John Byrne Collection; p. 33 AFP/Getty Images; p. 36 SPL/Science Source; p. 43 Chicago Tribune/Tribune News Service/Getty Images; p. 45 The Washington Times/ZumaPress.com; p. 46 Library of Congress Prints and Photographs Division; back cover and interior pages (binary numbers pattern) © iStockphoto .com/Vjom; interior pages (numbers and letters pattern) © iStockphoto.com/maxkabakov.

Designer: Matt Cauli; Senior Editor: Kathy Kuhtz Campbell; Photo Researcher: Bruce Donnola